A NOTE TO PARENTS ABOUT BEING WASTEFUL

"Waste not, want not." This saying is as relevant today as it was when it originated many years ago. What is known today that was not well known then is that wastefulness is more than a threat to human desire. It is a threat to human life because it can often be harmful to the environment.

The purpose of this book is to teach children the importance of conserving food, water, clothes, fuel, supplies, and money. It also teaches children concrete things they can do to conserve these valuable resources.

Most families are confronted with the problem of waste. By reading and discussing this book with your child, you can help him or her become part of the solution rather than part of the problem. You can help your child conserve, rather than waste, your family's resources.

It is important to acknowledge the conservation efforts made by your child. Thank him or her for remembering to turn off the lights. Praise him or her for not taking more food than he or she can eat. Celebrate decreased utility bills with a special family treat or outing. Above all, compliment any attempt to avoid waste.

This book belongs to:

_____

Published by Scholastic Inc.
90 Old Sherman Turnpike, Danbury, CT 06816.

SCHOLASTIC and associated logos are trademarks and/or
registered trademarks of Scholastic Inc.

ISBN 0-7172-8587-1

First Scholastic Printing, October 2005

A Book About
Being Wasteful

by **Joy Berry**

SCHOLASTIC INC.

New York   Toronto   London   Auckland   Sydney
Mexico City   New Delhi   Hong Kong   Buenos Aires

This is a book about Katie.

Reading about Katie can help you understand and deal with **being wasteful.**

You are being wasteful when you use more of something than you need.

You are being wasteful when you damage
or destroy something.

Something that is wasted might be difficult or impossible to replace.

You might run out of something you need if you waste things.

Do not be wasteful or you might not have what you need.

You need many things to help you live every day. Here are some of the things you will most likely need:

- food
- water
- clothes
- fuel
- supplies
- money

You need *food* to help keep your body alive and well. Try not to waste it.

- Do not take more food than you can eat.
- Eat whatever food you take.
- Do not play with your food.

You need *water* to drink and to keep yourself clean.

- Do not waste it.
- Do not use more water than you need.
- Do not let water run from a faucet or hose unless you are using it.
- Do not leave a faucet dripping. Turn it off completely when you finish using it.

You need *clothes* to protect your body and help keep it warm. Try not to waste them.

- Avoid getting your clothes dirty. Dirt can ruin them. Clothes that must be cleaned often wear out faster.
- Do not damage your clothes.
- Do not lose your clothes.

You need *fuel for your home.* Fuel helps provide light so that you can see. It helps keep the temperature in your home comfortable. It runs the appliances you and your family use. Try not to waste fuel.

- Turn off the lights in rooms that no one is using.
- Do not turn on the heater or air conditioner unless you have permission.
- Turn off any appliance that is not being used.

You need *fuel to power the cars and buses* that take you where you need to go. Try not to waste it.

- Ask to be driven someplace only when it is necessary.
- Walk or ride a bike whenever possible.

You need *supplies* such as pencils, paper, toilet paper, soap, shampoo, and adhesive tape.

- Do not waste them.
- Do not use more of them than you need.

You need *money*. Money buys you the things you need and want. Try not to waste it.

- Do not buy things you are not going to use.
- Buy the things you need before you buy the things you want.
- Take care of your money. Do not lose it.

Being wasteful is not good for you or others.

Wastefulness can use up the valuable resources you need to survive and grow.

People are happier when they have the things they need. Be careful not to waste the things around you so that you and others will have whatever is needed.